A BOOT UP

WEST SUSSEX PUBS

PHIL CHRISTIAN

First published in Great Britain in 2015
Copyright text and photographs
© 2015 Phil Christian

British Library Cataloguing-in-Publication Data
A CIP record for this title is available from the
British Library

ISBN 978 0 85710 096 2

PiXZ Books
Halsgrove House, Ryelands Business Park,
Bagley Road, Wellington, Somerset TA21 9PZ
Tel: 01823 653777
Fax: 01823 216796
email: sales@halsgrove.com

An imprint of Halstar Ltd, part of the
Halsgrove group of companies
Information on all Halsgrove titles is available at:
www.halsgrove.com

Printed and bound in China by
Toppan Leefung Printing Ltd

Contents

How to use this book

The Area

West Sussex is a county in the south of England covering 1991 sq. km (769 sq. mi) which is bordered by East Sussex, Hampshire and Surrey. It has a wide range of scenery including Wealden (an area situated between the parallel chalk escarpments of the North and South Downs), Downland, rivers and coastal.

Chichester is the county town and the only city in West Sussex. The highest point in the county is Black Down (1 mile south of Haslemere near the Surrey border) at some 280m (919 ft.).

West Sussex has a number of stately homes and castles such as Arundel and Bramber. Over half of the county is protected countryside, which offers good walking, cycling and other recreational opportunities. The county also has a large number of lovely country pubs and this book features 27 of them over the 10 walks.

This book aims to combine two or three of these pubs on each walk that are conveniently reached via footpaths. The walks range from 2.75 miles to 9 miles, but don't let the longer ones deter you. They have been carefully selected so that they

give you a day out with plenty to see and do, so there is no rush. The routes are also designed to include as many other areas of interest as possible making the walks an enjoyable day out for everyone.

Other attractions visited in this book include: Wittering beaches, Chichester Harbour, churches, Arundel Castle, various bridges, Priest House Museum and a photographic challenge on Walk 9 to try and get that perfect close-up of a plane flying low overhead having just taken off from Gatwick.

Routes and Maps

All of the walks are circular so you conveniently end up back where you started. The routes have been described in fine detail but a compass and Ordnance Survey map is always recommended wherever you go walking.

Parking

Parking locations have been given for each walk. The parking is free on all the walks at the time of writing but please check to make sure that charges have not been introduced over time or any restrictions imposed.

Public Transport

Buses

Bus times for journeys across West Sussex and beyond are available from the Traveline website – www.traveline.info

You can also call Traveline on 0871 200 22 33.
Additional information, including online timetables, is available from the West Sussex County Council web-site at www.westsussex.gov.uk and follow their home page.

Southern Trains

Customer Services – open daily 6am till midnight (closed Christmas Day).

www.southernrailway.com or
Tel: 08451 27 29 20 Option 1

Enjoy the walks and don't forget your camera!

Key to Symbols Used

Level of difficulty:

Easy

Fair

Difficult

Map symbols:

⊟ Park & start

••••• Walk route

—— Road

—— Canal/water

▪▪▪▪ Railway line

▪ Building

+ Church

▲ Landmark

🪣 Pub

Walk Locations

9

10 EAST GRINSTEAD

7

6

8

4

EAST SUSSEX

WEST MARDEN

WEST SUSSEX

3

5

2

1

BRIGHTON

N
W E
S

1 East Wittering, West Itchenor & West Wittering (3 Pubs)

This 9 mile walk is almost entirely flat but the pebbles and sand on section 2 are heavy going and quite strenuous. There are lovely views across the sea, lovely pubs and an option to do a short detour to explore The Spit. The return route is along a number of quiet lanes which are quite welcoming after the effort used on section 2.

The walk begins by heading down to the beach beside the Shore Inn. From here you begin your lengthy walk along the pebbles of East Wittering beach and then across the famous fine sand of West Wittering beach which gets very busy on sunny days. At the end of West Wittering beach there is an option to do a short detour to explore The Spit before beginning the long coastal walk up

Level: 🥾 🥾 🥾
Length: 9 miles (14.5km)
Terrain: Although this walk is generally flat, section 2 along pebbles and sand is quite strenuous and the return route along quiet lanes is quite welcoming.
Stiles: 0
Park & start: Roadside parking in Culimore Road or other side road. Alternatively, there is a pay-and display car park in Marine Drive.
Postcode: PO20 8HB
Start ref: SZ 792971
Refreshments: Featured pubs and various in East Wittering.

to West Itchenor where you can enjoy well deserved refreshments in the

Chichester Channel

Boatyard

Ship Inn

St Nicholas Church

Ella Nore

Lamb Inn

The Spit

West Wittering

B2179

t Wittering Beach

East Wittering Beach

East Wittering

Shore Inn

Ship Inn. The return journey has been deliberately chosen to use a few fairly quiet lanes as your legs will notice the effort used on section 2. The final part of the walk is across fields and through a camp site back to the start.

(1) From the lower house number end of Culimore Road go left along Marine Drive and follow it past a green on the left and then a pay-and-display car park (alternative parking area). At the end, go right

The Shore Inn

East Wittering beach – Spinnaker Tower ahead

down Shore Road, not signed, and near the end you reach the Shore Inn on the right.

(2) From the pub, continue down Shore Road to the beach and turn right by the Fisherman's Hut and walk along the concrete path. Soon the path ends and you have to continue along the top of the pebble beach

with a view of the Spinnaker Tower at Portsmouth in view ahead. Just follow the beach along concrete, pebbles or grass ignoring any of the exits on the right.

As you walk into a grassy area, with your view of the sea obscured you start to get the sense that you are starting to walk on fine sand and as you continue to climb a bank and go along a sandy roped-off path you arrive at the famous and very popular sandy West Wittering beach – no pebbles.

Continue along the top of the beach, passing beach huts on the right with a large visitor car park behind them. Just keep going to the end of the beach where there are a few more pebbles and now you have arrived at the start of The Spit. You can go and explore The Spit as an optional detour but my walk continues to the next pub which is still a few miles away.

(3) Turn right at the end of the beach heading towards the end of the car park. Just before the car park entrance go left with a low wooden fence on your right. Follow the enclosed path, which is shared with cyclists, enjoying some lovely views of The Spit and boats on your left as you go.

The Spit

WEST WITTERING

West Wittering, famous for its unspoilt sandy beaches, lies near the mouth of Chichester Harbour. It has the highest standard of water quality and with its excellent facilities is regarded as one of the premier Blue Flag beaches in the country. For such a small village it has been the home to some notable residents including Keith Richards of the Rolling Stones, actor Nicholas Lyndhurst and Sir Henry Royce the engineer and designer of Rolls-Royce cars and aero-engines.

Cross a bridge and in a few yards you reach a 3-way signpost; you are now at Snow Hill, keep left here and continue with the sea view. In a few yards you reach a 4-way footpath sign and again you keep left nearest to the sea. Follow the enclosed path as it winds its way offering some open views of the sea as you go.

At a bird hide the path bends to the right, you are now at Ella Nore. Continue following the path, go through a gate and immediately go left through another gate and continue beside the sea. At a 2-way footpath sign, with a wide gate on the left, go right as directed, then left and ahead through a swing gate and follow the enclosed path back to the sea. Continue, ignoring any side

paths and crossing a few bridges as you go.

After what seems like forever, you reach a boatyard. Walk directly ahead across the boatyard and continue along the enclosed path on the other side.

On the far side you reach the Harbour Office at West Itchenor; here you can go on Harbour Tours around Chichester Harbour. Turn right up The Street, not signed and in about 50 yards you reach the Ship Inn on the right for well-deserved refreshments.

WEST ITCHENOR

Itchenor boatyards are almost as old as the village and were recorded as providing ships for the Napoleonic wars. In WWII, landing craft were constructed here which took part in the D-Day landings in 1944. Today the boatyard has a more upmarket clientele and it constructs and fits out luxury yachts.

CHICHESTER CHANNEL AND HARBOUR

Chichester Harbour is a large natural harbour to the south west of Chichester on the Solent which straddles West Sussex and Hampshire. The harbour and surrounding land is managed by Chichester Harbour Conservancy. The tidal flats are of outstanding ecological significance and very large populations of wildfowl and waders use the mudflats feeding on the rich plant life and the huge population of intertidal invertebrates. Over 7,500 Brent geese overwinter here or on adjacent farmland and over 50,000 birds reside in or visit the harbour throughout the year. This is one of the south coast's most popular sailing waters with up to 12,500 craft regularly using the harbour, with competitive racing taking place among the 14 sailing clubs of the Chichester Harbour Federation.

The Ship Inn

4   Leave the pub and turn right down The Street. The fairly quiet road soon passes St Nicholas church on the left and a pond on the right. Just follow what has now become Itchenor Road, ignoring any side roads or footpaths. At a main road junction go right signposted to Witterings.

East Wittering, West Itchenor & West Wittering

Follow the road and in a short distance, where it curves to the right, go almost directly ahead along a footpath on the left as directed by a footpath sign (this is on the bend). Follow the path which can get overgrown, cross a wooden bridge and at the end you reach a main road. Turn left along the road for a few yards to reach the Lamb Inn on the left.

The Lamb Inn

Leave the pub and taking care; go right along the main road using the right hand grass verge. When you reach Itchenor Road, cross over the main road and go along Piggery Hall Lane opposite. At a road junction, go right along Acre Street. At the end, go left down Chapel Lane, not signed, and when the road curves right, by a low-level sign on the left for Elms Lane, go left at a wide opening as directed by a footpath sign.

Follow the obvious path across a large field, cross a bridge and continue directly ahead across a field. On the far side, go ahead along a path through a camp site. When you reach a main building continue ahead passing through a gap to the right of a wide metal gate. Then pass to the left of a wide metal gate and continue ahead along an access road to reach a road at the end.

Turn left along the road and just before a sign for East Wittering, go right down The Crescent. At the end by house no. 43 go right along a 'T' road, pass between a barrier and follow Culimore Road ahead and around to the left back to the start.

2 **Chidham & Nutbourne** (3 Pubs)

This 7.5 mile walk is completely flat. For most of the walk there are lovely coastal views across Bosham and Thorney Channels

and the walk visits three lovely pubs. There is one short section of beach walking on section 5 that can be difficult /perhaps impossible at the highest of highest tides so you may want to check on-line before you start; however this is very unlikely to affect you.

The walk begins by the lovely Old House at Home pub, which I recommend you save until the end of the walk. From here it is not that far until you reach the Barleycorn pub and a little further on the Bosham Inn; two lovely pubs. You then start your walk around the perimeter of Chidham, beside the Bosham

Level:
Length: 7.5 miles (12 km)
Terrain: This is a completely level walk. There is one short section along pebbles and one area where the ground is uneven.
Stiles: 0
Park & start: Roadside parking by the Old House at Home pub.
Postcode: PO18 8SU
Start ref: SU 786040
Refreshments: Featured pubs.

then Thorney Channels; this is the highlight of the walk. Look out for numerous boats, wading birds, butterflies and lizards as you go. The walk ends back at the Old House at Home and believe me you will be ready for refreshments.

The Barley Corn
Bosham Inn
Old House at Home
Chidham
Holy Trinity
Activity Centre
orney annel

Chidham & Nutbourne

13

CHIDHAM

A recent excavation has shown that man used Chidham more than 4000 years ago. The flint scrapers found on the site on the western shore of the peninsula, suggest that spear shafts or kiddles (fish traps) and primitive salterns (area used for salt making) were being made here. It is believed that the Saxon Saint Cuthman may have been born here around 681.

The Old House at Home

1 With your back to the pub, which I recommend you visit at the end or both, go left up Cot Lane. Just follow the quiet lane to reach a road at the end with the Barleycorn pub on the left.

The Barleycorn

2 Turn right along the main road and cross over as soon as possible. Soon you reach the lovely Bosham Inn on the left hand side.

The Bosham Inn

Leave the pub, cross over the road, and go left continuing along the main road. Just before a white building go right at a footpath sign with the Bosham Channel on your left.

3 Now just follow the obvious perimeter path beside the channel admiring the views but taking care as the path can be a little uneven and overgrown in places. For part of the walk your view of the channel is blocked by a high bank next to you but that soon ends.

BOSHAM AND THORNEY CHANNELS

Bosham & Thorney Channels form part of Chichester Harbour, a Site of Special Scientific Interest (SSSI). It is a wetland of international importance, a Special Protection Area for wild birds and a Special Area of Conservation. The harbour is of particular importance for wintering wildfowl and waders as five species reach numbers which are internationally important.

The path curves to the right and reaches a lane. Go left along the lane passing a pond on the right. Just after the pond go left along Harbour Way as directed by a 3-way signpost. Go along this Pedestrian Only access staying strictly on the access road.

At a grass roundabout go ahead on an enclosed path as directed by a 2-way footpath sign. Soon you arrive back beside the channel with the Holy Trinity church at Bosham Quay clearly in view across the channel.

4 Continue around the edge of the channel on a raised bank and at a 3-way signpost keep left on the perimeter path. Keep a look out for wading birds and continue to

reach a boat-shaped activity centre. Go right down steps and across a plank bridge. Follow the path around the back of the activity centre,

cross an access road and continue almost directly ahead across a plank bridge as directed by a 2-way footpath sign.

Holy Trinity church at Bosham Quay

CHIDHAM

During the nineteenth century the men of Chidham appeared to have been farmers rather than fishermen or sailors, probably due to the good quality of the soil. In 1812 an embankment wall was constructed from Chidham to Bosham where use was made of an old quay. Writing of Bosham in the 1860s Charles Longcroft described how the newly enclosed land was ploughed and planted with corn. He wrote, 'But one November, there came a raging tide and a gale wind, from the southwest and away went the embankment.' In 1825 the sea returned covering the farmland and inundating new buildings. One of these buildings is said to have been a mansion, standing at Cutmill whose stone was then used to build Cutmill Cottage.

Little egret

At the next 2-way sign you go left back down to the channel edge and continue around the perimeter.

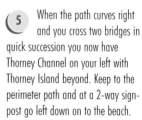

5 When the path curves right and you cross two bridges in quick succession you now have Thorney Channel on your left with Thorney Island beyond. Keep to the perimeter path and at a 2-way signpost go left down on to the beach.

Continue along the beach, which can be tricky at the highest of high tides, and pass a bird hide on the way.

After a few hundred yards, when the beach starts to curve around to the right, you step to the right and continue on a raised bank for a few yards. At the start of a fence, go right on a well-trodden path as directed by an Alternative Footpath sign; at the time of writing the onward perimeter path had been badly damaged by storms and was not likely to be repaired.

Go ahead across the grass area with a dip / stream a few yards to your right and New Barn beyond. Just follow the path next to the dip and eventually you arrive back at the channel edge.

Continue ahead and soon you reach a 3-way footpath sign where you turn sharply right, back on yourself, down six steps. Follow the field edge then go left around the right field edge and on across the centre of two fields.

Cross a plank bridge and continue ahead on the clear path to reach Cot Lane used on the outward journey. Turn right along the lane back to the start and well-deserved refreshment at the Old House at Home.

Beach beside Thorney Channel

3 **Charlton & Singleton** (2 Pubs)

This is one of the shortest walks that I have ever written but it is still very enjoyable and could be combined with another walk in the book. The walk focuses on two lovely pubs in two equally lovely small, remote country villages with good elevated views of both villages between the two.

The walk begins by the Fox Goes Free pub then climbs quite steeply up on to Levin Down where you are rewarded with good views of both Charlton and Singleton. The descent takes you into Singleton where you can visit the Partridge Inn or alternatively take tea and perhaps a breakfast or lunch in Singleton Tea

Level: 🥾 🥾
Length: 2.75 miles (4.4 km)
Terrain: A hilly outward journey; then downhill with a level return.
Stiles: 1
Park & start: Roadside parking by the Fox Goes Free.
Postcode: PO18 0HU
Start ref: SU 887129
Refreshments: The Fox Goes Free, the Partridge Inn and Singleton Tea Rooms.

Rooms. The return journey takes you past the Blessed Virgin Mary church then across a field with good views to the left of your elevated outward journey.

19

CHARLTON

Charlton is famous for The Charlton Hunt which began in the 1670s and is the earliest documented pack of hounds to hunt fox alone. The hunt became popular among the gentry and has never been equalled. Since the reign of Charles II almost every noble family in the land had a representative at Charlton, including almost half of the Knights of the Garter. Its first proprietor was the Duke of Monmouth and it was the first hunt to establish a club. The local pub, the Fox Goes Free, commemorates this activity. It is also the location where the first Women's Institute in England held its inaugural meeting during the First World War.

The Fox Goes Free

1 With the pub on your right, walk along the pavement and continue to a road junction. Continue ahead along the road and in about 35 yards, where there are speed restriction signs painted on the road, go right through a swing gate. Follow the clear path steeply up across the field with good views of Singleton away to your left.

At the top go through two gates on to Levin Down by a 3-way signpost and a Levin Down information board. Follow the footpath to the left of the information board and continue to climb diagonally with good elevated views of Charlton and Singleton on the left. Soon you pass through another gate and continue to climb diagonally before the path levels off.

2 Ignore a gate on the left and continue for a few more yards and go through two swing gates. Continue ahead but slightly left and downhill and you will soon notice that the path curves left towards a gate which is in sight in the hedgerow ahead. Go through the gate, ahead, and through another gate. From here it is downhill across the field heading towards Singleton.

Towards the bottom you walk with a row of trees / bushes on your right and at the bottom you go through another gate. Pass a small graveyard on the right and go out to a road.

Turn right along the road passing the Village Hall on your left. Follow the road around to the right passing some lovely thatched houses. Cross a picturesque stream and at a junction you reach a stone building which is a popular Tea Rooms that sells breakfasts, lunches, cream teas, homemade cakes etc. Just before the Tea Rooms, go left along a road, signposted to The Parish Church and The Playground. Go to the end to reach the Partridge Inn on the left.

SINGLETON

The name Singleton derives from the Anglo-Saxon 'sengel', which means 'burnt clearing'. The Weald and Downland Open Air Museum of Historic Buildings is on the edge of the village. Here there are over 40 historic buildings from South East England which have been rescued from destruction, dismantled, then reconstructed on the site.

Singleton

Singleton tea rooms

The Partridge Inn

(3) Leave the pub and go left along the road. In a few yards go right along a T-Road, passing some lovely stone houses, to reach the church of the Blessed Virgin Mary in view ahead.

The Blessed Virgin Mary church

Just before the church entrance, go left through the church car park and on past a children's play area. In the far left corner go ahead past houses as directed by public footpath arrows. Continue ahead along a short road, cross a road, and then continue directly ahead between houses along an enclosed public footpath.

Go through a gate and ahead across a large field with good views on your left of where you walked on the outward journey. Just keep walking directly ahead on the faint path with the buildings at Charlton ahead getting gradually closer. On the far side of the field, go slightly to the right and cross the stile to the left of a large metal gate out to a road.

Go directly ahead along the road opposite between houses. Follow it when it bends around to the left, passing a phone box, to arrive back at the pub at the start.

View of outward route

4 **Tillington & Petworth** (2 Pubs)

This 4.5 mile walk is fairly easy going even though there are a few hills; they are gentle climbs and the rest of the walk is along well defined tracks / quiet roads. There is one path along Hungers Lane which is uneven due to water erosion so extra care is needed here.

The walk begins by the Horse Guards Inn / All Hallows church and heads down quiet lanes / tracks to cross the River Rother. From here it is a pleasant walk to reach Badgers pub by Coultershaw Bridge. The first part of the return journey re-traces your outward journey but then continues along

Level: ♥ ♥
Length: 4.5 miles (7.2 km)
Terrain: This walk has a few hills but they are all gentle climbs. Take care along Hungers Lane as the path has been eroded by water.
Stiles: 0
Park & start: On road parking near the Horse Guards Inn.
Postcode: GU28 9AF
Start ref: SU 962220
Refreshments: The Horse Guards Inn and Badgers Inn.

the interesting Hungers Lane which is an ancient path with high stone banks on either side with a network of tree roots that work their way down through the rock; the trees themselves

23

overhang the path in precarious positions and the path is very uneven due to water erosion. The final part of the walk takes you back to All Hallows church with its famous Scots Crown Spire.

① With your back to the pub, go right down the road to reach the main A272 at the end. Cross the road and continue ahead down the quiet T road opposite. Just follow the road as it descends, passing farm

buildings and soon with the benefit of some good views.

When you reach a house directly in front of you with a marker post on the right, go right and in a few yards the road becomes a track. In 40 yards, at another marker post, go across the middle of a field aiming for trees on the other side.

At a 2-way footpath sign, go left and in 20 yards at another 2-way footpath

sign, continue along a left field edge. In the field corner, go through a wide metal gate by a marker post and turn left along a wide access track. Pass through a farm and then immediately go right at a marker post to cross a bridge, which is in view, over the River Rother.

On the other side of the bridge, go through a gate and continue ahead up a wide access track / road. When you reach a marker post on the left,

THE HORSE GUARDS INN

The Horse Guards Inn is a 350 year old pub in the South Downs National Park. It is thought to have got its name in the 1840s from the cavalry who stayed there whilst their horses rested on the grass of Petworth Estate under the watchful eye of Lord Egremont.

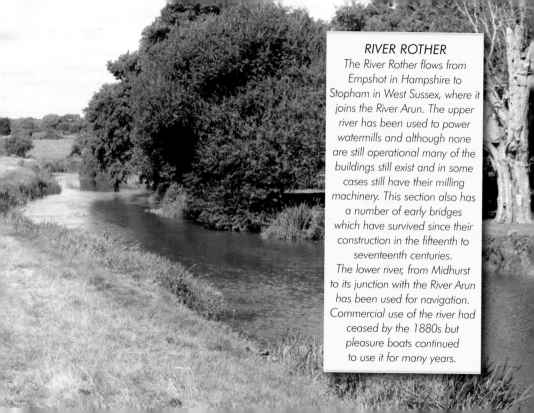

RIVER ROTHER

The River Rother flows from Empshot in Hampshire to Stopham in West Sussex, where it joins the River Arun. The upper river has been used to power watermills and although none are still operational many of the buildings still exist and in some cases still have their milling machinery. This section also has a number of early bridges which have survived since their construction in the fifteenth to seventeenth centuries.

The lower river, from Midhurst to its junction with the River Arun has been used for navigation. Commercial use of the river had ceased by the 1880s but pleasure boats continued to use it for many years.

continue ahead and climb gently with a view of Badgers Inn on your left, to reach a main road at the end.

Now, taking great care, go left along the road using its right hand side and cross a bridge to reach an access road by the pub. Before visiting the pub turn right along the access road for a few yards to view the Old Railway Station guest accommodation where guests actually get to stay in Pullman railway carriages (what a lovely place to stay). Now return back along the road to visit Badgers Inn.

2 Leave the pub, go left back along the road and turn right back along the access road you used to get here. Follow the road, re-tracing your outward path, passing

The Old Railway Station

the marker post on the right and continue until you re-cross the River Rother.

On the other side of the river you reach a marker post; go ahead here with a low wooden fence on your right. When the fence ends, go ahead for a few yards to reach a 3-way bridleway sign on the left. Taking care because the ground is very uneven due to water erosion, go left up an interesting path, Hungers Lane, with high stone banks on either side with a network of tree roots growing down through them.

Just follow this track ahead, climbing gently and passing a crossing point on the way. At the top you reach the busy A272 with Petworth Park

Hungers Lane

opposite. Cross the road, turn left and follow the road around to the left with the stone wall of Petworth Park on your right and a good view of All Hallows church beyond.

When the road bends to the left, keep the stone wall on your right and follow the footpath beside the wall which takes you back to All Hallows church / the Horse Guards Inn at the start.

ALL HALLOWS CHURCH

The tower of All Hallows church was re-built in 1807 surmounted with the now famous 'Scots Crown spire' which is flood-lit at night. The tower houses five bells, three of which are dated 1572, 1622 and 1651.

5 Burpham, Arundel & Offham (3 Pubs)

This 8.75 mile walk is mainly flat. There is a climb at the start and at the end of the walk and 23 stiles to cross. The walk is all about the River Arun and the views of Arundel Castle which dominates the skyline as well as the pubs featured on this walk.

The walk begins by the George at Burpham and soon descends down to the River Arun via the steps of Jacob's Ladder. The rest of the walk, with the exception of a detour to visit the Red Lion in Arundel, is along the raised river-bank of the River Arun. En-route you visit the lovely and very popular Black Rabbit pub and before you start your return journey you can visit St

Level: 🐾 🐾
Length: 8.75 miles (14km)
Terrain: This walk is mainly level with short climbs at the start and end.
Stiles: 23
Park & start: Village car park behind the pub / beside the Village Hall.
Postcode: BN18 9RR
Start ref: TQ 039089
Refreshments: Featured pubs and various in Arundel.

Leonard's church in the little village of South Stoke.

1 From the car park go back to the George at Burpham pub and opposite it is the church of St Mary the Virgin if you wish to visit it.

The George

BURPHAM

Burpham and the surrounding area has yielded Iron Age and Neolithic remains including the bones of an elephant near Peppering Farm. The village is next to the site of a Saxon Burh (an Old English term for "fortification") with earthworks to protect against Viking attack up the River Arun. Folklore has it that nearby Harrow Hill was the last place in Britain where fairies lived, until disturbed by archaeologists. The village has a century-old cricket pitch where W.G. Grace played. Jacob's Ladder leads from the top of the hill where there was once a Saxon hill fort (where the cricket ground and village hall are now) to the riverbank below, which was very useful in the time of smugglers. They would land their booty on the riverbank and carry it up to the top where the old fort had been sited and on to the conveniently located seventeenth century George pub.

From the pub, go left back towards the car park as directed by a footpath sign on the right, but do not go to the car park instead head out across a playing field passing the Village Hall on your left.

On the far side go to the left of a children's play area and go through a swing gate. Go ahead along an enclosed path which can get a little overgrown. Soon you arrive at Jacob's Ladder, which used to be used by smugglers, go down 78 steps to

Cows, railway line and castle

reach a stile by a 3-way footpath sign. Go over the stile and ahead towards the River Arun which is obscured by vegetation for quite a while.

(2) Now keep walking, crossing a number of stiles on the way and soon Arundel Castle appears on the skyline ahead of you. Just keep going, cross a railway line via two stiles and continue ahead, soon on a raised bank aiming for the Black Rabbit pub which is in view but on the other side of the river — you visit it later. At the time of writing (and it's obviously been here for a long time) there was a boat wreck here which at least makes for an interesting photograph.

Continue left around the raised bank, crossing more stiles and soon you get your first view of the River Arun. Now just keep going beside the river to the very end of this riverbank path where you arrive at the back end of a car park. Go directly ahead between houses to a road and turn right over the river; from here you get a good view of Blackfriars ruins of a Dominican priory. At a mini round-about, go ahead up the High Street and soon you reach the Red Lion pub

The Black Rabbit across the river

ARUNDEL

Arundel town is a major bridging point over the River Arun and was the lowest road bridge until the opening of the Littlehampton swing bridge in 1908. Arundel Castle was built by the Normans to protect that vulnerable point to the north of the valley through the South Downs. The castle is a restored medieval castle. It was founded by Roger de Montgomery on Christmas Day 1067. He became the first to hold the Earldom of Arundel by the grace of William the Conqueror. The castle was damaged in the English Civil War and restored in the eighteenth and nineteenth centuries.

Arundel Castle

The Red Lion

which is on the left behind the war memorial.

3 Leave the pub and go back down the High Street to the mini roundabout. Go left passing Blackfriars ruins of a Dominican priory on the right and the entrance to Arundel Castle on the left.

When you are level with the castle entrance go right opposite it into a car park beside a museum. Pass the

BLACKFRIARS OR DOMINICAN FRIARY

The Blackfriars or Dominican Friary was founded in the second quarter of the thirteenth century perhaps by Isabel, Countess of Arundel. Friars liked to live close to the people they were preaching to and here they were beside not only the river crossing but also the port and market.

Waterside Tea Garden on the right and in a few more yards go right up a bank to re-join the river, now on the other side. Now just follow the path beside the river and just keep on going until you eventually reach the Black Rabbit pub.

The Black Rabbit

RIVER ARUN

The River Arun is sourced from a series of small streams in the St Leonard's Forest area, east of Horsham. After flowing through Horsham to the west, it is joined by the North River at Nowhurst. Turning to the south it is joined by its main tributary the western River Rother and continues through Arundel, past Arundel Castle to join the English Channel at Littlehampton. It is one of the faster flowing rivers in England and is tidal as far inland as Pallingham Quay which is 25.5 miles (41 km) upstream from the sea at Littlehampton. Along its bank at Offham near Arundel Castle is the popular Black Rabbit pub which gets very busy in the summer especially with walkers who enjoy a drink beside the river.

(4) Leave the pub, turn left through their car park and at its end continue through trees then on beside the riverbank. Pass a green metal bridge and continue towards the little church of St Leonard at South Stoke in view ahead. At South Stoke, cross a stile beside the bridge and either go left to visit the church or go across the bridge to continue the walk – go to section 5. To visit the church go left up the access road and just after you round a bend to the left

Church of St Leonard

the access to the church is on your left. Return to the bridge after your visit.

(5) Cross the bridge and immediately go right over a stile and again follow the riverbank path which can get a little overgrown in places. Just stay beside the riverbank until you naturally re-cross the railway line via two more stiles.

Continue ahead on the clear wide grassy path which curves gradually to the right with Peppering Farm in view ahead; near here the bones of an elephant have been found.

At a 3-way footpath sign, go ahead through a wide gate and immediately keep right to a stile in view to the

Bridge at South Stoke

right of a metal gate. Cross the stile and go ahead across a field with the river still on your right. On the far side of the field, go through a metal swing gate and go ahead climbing quite steeply and taking care as there is a steep drop on your right hand side. At a 2-way footpath sign go left and climb with a wooden fence on your left and then a stone wall. The George pub is a few yards further on back at the start.

This walk is fairly easy going although there are a couple of minor climbs. It is mainly across fields and along quiet lanes and there is a lot to see, especially if you like bridges.

The walk begins beside the cricket green which does have signs warning you of the possible damage that could be caused to your car if you park there when cricket is going to be played, I assume that would score a 6. You then reach the Three Crowns pub before heading past the village pond and church on your way to the River Arun and the Wey & Arun Canal. A large part of the walk is now beside one or both of

Level: 🥾 🥾
Length: 5.75 miles (9.3km)
Terrain: Mainly level across fields between the River Arun and the Wey & Arun Canal.
Stiles: 10
Park & start: By the cricket green in Durbans Road.
Postcode: RH14 0DG
Start ref: TQ 049262
Refreshments: Featured pubs.

these water features and you pass a few bridges on your way to the Bat & Ball pub. The last part of the walk is along a quiet road, passing Fishers Adventure Park land, on your way to the Cricketers Arms back at the start.

Map labels:
5
Bridge
4
Bat & Ball
cket een
Cricketer's Arms
Lift Bridge
1
The Three Crowns
St Peter ad Vincula
New Bridge
3
borough reen
Wey & Arun Canal
er Bird
Lock Waterwheel
River Arun
2
Floodgate Bridge

WISBOROUGH GREEN

Wisborough Green is focused around the large village green which is around 9 acres in size. The British Lawn Mower Racing Association (BLMRA) was founded in 1973 at the Cricketers Arms by a man named Jim Gavin, an Irishman who had raced cars across the world. He became disillusioned with the increasing costs of motor sport so he got together with a group of locals to create a cheap form of motor sport that was accessible to all. A 12 hour race is held locally at Brinsbury College near Pullborough with a weekend of frantic racing held at the Bat & Ball pub in October.

The Three Crowns

Village pond

① Go along Durbans Road back to the main A272; turn left and you immediately reach the Three Crowns pub.

Leave the pub and go left, crossing School Road and passing the picturesque village pond. Continue along the road using the left hand pavement and soon you pass the church of St Peter ad Vincula perched up on your left.

When you reach Glebe Way, cross the main road and go right down an access road which is also a public bridleway. Follow the access road, crossing the River Kird on the way to reach its end by Harsfold Farmhouse on the left. Continue ahead along the gravel track and in a short distance, by a 2-

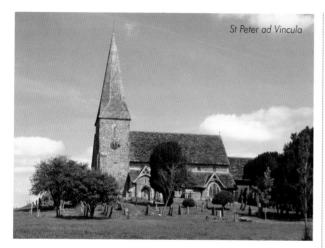

St Peter ad Vincula

(2) Go left over the stile and walk with the Wey & Arun Canal (disused) on your right. Follow the path beside the generally obscured canal, pass through a squeeze stile and continue until you cross Lording's Bridge and flood gate.

Turn left, now on other side of the canal and stay on this path soon crossing two bridges. Go through a swing gate on your right and turn left

way footpath sign, continue ahead passing outbuildings on the left.

Continue ahead, descending very gradually and at a 3-way footpath sign keep going ahead. Go through a

bridle gate and continue to pass through a wide metal gate and cross a bridge over the River Arun. Continue ahead and soon you reach a stile on the left with a 4-way footpath sign 3 yards further on.

Lording's Bridge and flood gates

WEY & ARUN CANAL

The Wey & Arun Canal is a 23 mile long (37 km) canal between the River Wey at Shalford, Surrey and the River Arun at Pallingham in West Sussex. The canal comprises parts of two separate undertakings – the northern part of the Arun Navigation, between Pallingham and Newbridge Wharf, which opened in 1787, and the Wey & Arun Junction Canal, which connected the Arun at Newbridge to the Godalming Navigation near Shalford, south of Guildford, which opened in 1816. The canal was built with 26 locks.

Lording's Lock

Lording's Waterwheel

to cross a bridge by a 3-way footpath sign. On the other side of the bridge you reach Lording's Lock and Lording's Waterwheel.

Continue on the path ahead, soon crossing a stile and then following the clear, winding grassy path with a row of trees a few yards over on your left.

In the far corner, cross a stile and continue now with the canal on your right again. Just follow the path, crossing a stile that has uneven footings on the other side due to tree roots, as you go. Soon the canal bends away to the right but you continue ahead with a row of trees on your left, taking care here as it is uneven underfoot.

In the far corner, go ahead over a wooden bridge and continue ahead / left for 25 yards to reach a 4-way footpath sign on the left. Go ahead here, cross a stile and continue ahead with the canal on your left. Soon you curve left, between river and canal, cross a stile and go on to reach the A272 at New Bridge.

(3) Go through a wide gate, cross the road and continue along the footpath opposite. Cross a stile, continue between river and canal and just keep on going, passing Northlands Lift Bridge on the way and crossing a couple of stiles. Eventually you reach a bridge over the canal by a 4-way footpath sign, but as far as I am aware this bridge is not named.

Northlands Lift Bridge

New Bridge

Bridge over Wey & Arun Canal

4 Go left over the bridge and almost immediately at a 2-way bridleway sign go right across the lower end of the field to another 2-way bridleway sign where you go left as directed up the right field edge. In the far right hand corner, go

through a wide metal gate and continue up a track as directed by a 2-way bridleway sign that is partly hidden in the right hand hedgerow. At Paplands Farm continue ahead up the access road to reach a road at the end.

Cross the road and follow Newpound Lane opposite, signed to Fishers Farm. Soon you reach the Bat & Ball pub on the left.

5 Leave the pub and return to Newpound Lane. Go left down the lane passing Fishers Adventure Farm Park on the left and just continue until you reach a road junction by the cricket green, the Cricketers Arms pub is to the right and your car is to the left.

The Bat & Ball

The Cricketers Arms

7 Barns Green, Two Mile Ash & Southwater (3 Pubs)

This his 7.75 mile walk is mainly flat across fields and along quiet lanes / tracks. There is one climb near the end but you are rewarded with a good view of the grounds of Christ's Hospital School, which you have just walked past.

The walk begins by the Queens Head pub and heads out down a road before continuing cross country on your way to the Bax Castle pub which is situated on the Downs Link bridle-way, making it very popular with walkers and cyclists. From here you continue to the Hen & Chicken pub before going through the grounds of Christ's Hospital School.

Level: 🥾 🥾 🥾
Length: 7.75 miles (12.5km)
Terrain: This is a fairly level walk although there is a climb near the end.
Stiles: 20
Park & start: Roadside parking near the Queens Head pub.
Postcode: RH13 0PS
Start ref: TQ 126270
Refreshments: Featured pubs

The return journey begins by crossing the railway, and then there is a steady climb with good views before finishing the walk by walking across Barns Green.

■ Christ's Hospital School

4

3 The Hen & Chicken

ns Green

1 The Queen's Head

2 Bax Castle

BARNS GREEN

Barns Green is a village about 2.5 miles north of Billingshurst. The village is noted for its annual winter half marathon race, of the same name, which is held at the end of October or beginning of November and is run on a looped course around the lanes surrounding the village.

With your back to the pub, go right along the road and at a road junction with Barns Green on the left, go right down Two Mile Ash Road. Go down the road, pass beneath a railway bridge and follow the winding road until you reach a footpath on the left directly opposite Trout Lane on the right.

Go over the stile and follow a left field edge with trees on your left. Cross a stile in the far corner out to an access road by a 3-way footpath sign. Turn right along the road and when it bends sharply to the right, by Rye Cottage on the left, go ahead beside Rye Cottage as directed by a 4-way footpath sign that is partly hidden in trees on the left.

Cross a stile and turn right by a wooden fence; cross more stiles and go through electric fences as you continue along the right edge of paddocks. At

The Queens Head

the end of the paddocks cross a stile and a sleeper bridge, then go left at a 2-way footpath sign. Follow the left field edge as it curves around to the right. In the far corner, go ahead for 3 yards to reach a wide path by a 3-way footpath sign beneath trees.

Go left along the path, pass a wide wooden gate and continue ahead along a wide grassy path. At a 3-way footpath sign just short of houses ahead, go right through a wide metal gate. Go diagonally across the field to the left of a power pole aiming for a stile in the hedgerow opposite. Cross the stile with care as it is uneven on the other side and go ahead across the middle of the next field which may have crops growing.

Aim for a wide gap in the hedgerow opposite and go diagonally left across the next field as directed by a foot-path sign in the hedge opening, again this field may have crops growing. Leave the field at its left corner, via a wide metal gate that is beside a brick outhouse, to reach a road.

Go left along the road, taking care as there is not much of a verge. Stay on this road and follow it around to the right, then it goes left over a bridge still on Two Mile Ash Road; the Bax Castle pub is a few yards down this road.

(2) Leave the pub and go back to the road by the pub entrance and turn right for 2 yards. At a foot-path sign on the left, go right along a

TWO MILE ASH

Two Mile Ash is a tiny village between Barns Green and Southwater. It is surrounded by countryside and farms with only a smattering of residences. It is best known for the Bax Castle public house which is next to the Downs Link bridleway and makes it very popular with walkers and cyclists.

Bax Castle

gravel drive between houses. Cross a stile and go ahead across a field on a faint path aiming for a wide metal gate in a gap in the trees opposite.

Cross a stile beside the gate and continue ahead up the next field again on a faint path near to the left hand field edge. In the far left field corner, go left over a stile and follow the path through trees and soon at an exit point on the right go over a stile and ahead up a left field edge.

Go over a stile in the field corner and immediately left along a field edge. Cross a stile in the corner and go right, then cross another stile out to a road. Go left along the road and at a mini roundabout continue ahead using the right hand pavement until

SOUTHWATER

Much of the population used to rely on the brick industry which thrived in the clay-pits up until the 1980s. After the closure of the brickworks there was a project implemented to transform the area into a country park, which is now one of the major family attractions in the district. In 2006 the centre of Southwater village was renewed at a cost of £25 million and this investment attracted substantial local business interest and improved the village for local residents. The amenities in the Lintot Square are now appropriate for the size of the village and include the unusually named Lintot pub. The name is a reference to Barnaby Bernard Lintot (1675 – 1736) an early English publisher who was born in Southwater.

The Hen & Chicken

you reach the Hen & Chicken on the right.

(3) Leave the pub, continue right along the road and just before it bends left go left at a bridleway sign. Follow the enclosed path

between trees / bushes and at its end you reach a road. Go left and in a few yards go right at a bridleway sign. Follow the concrete path with Christ's Hospital School on the right. At a junction, go left and follow the access road by playing fields.

On the far side of the large playing area the road curves right; pass a 3-way bridleway sign and in a further 25 yards, go left at a 2-way bridleway sign along an enclosed path beneath trees. At the end of the path, go ahead for a few yards then go left,

Christ's Hospital School

signposted Downs Link and with a railway line on your right.

In about 50 yards you pass a secluded house on the left and in another 30 yards, go right up steps to reach a 4-way footpath sign by a swing gate. Go ahead, cross a stile and go over the railway. Cross a stile on the other side and go ahead into woodland. Follow the winding path through the woods and on the far side climb four steps and leave the woodland.

Go ahead and climb up the right edge of a field with trees on the right. At the top, where the trees end continue ahead to the right of a solitary tree with good views of Christ's Hospital School on the right; you can see just how large this school is. Once past the solitary tree continue ahead between two fields, then on to cross a stile out to a road.

(4) Taking care, turn left along the fairly quiet road and soon, in about 100 yards, you reach Marlands on the left. Cross the road here and take the footpath opposite, which is just to the right of Storries, along a path through trees that can get a little overgrown. At the end you cross a stile out to an access track.

Go left along the track and just follow it soon passing Muntham Lodge and eventually reaching a gate ahead of you which is private for Muntham House School. Just before this gate, go left through a gate and diagonally right through woodland following a path to the left of the school grounds.

At a 4-way footpath sign, go left past a wide gate and ahead to cross a stile in a fence. Now you can go ahead across Barns Green to reach a road on the other side. Turn right along the road back to the Queens Head pub at the start.

Barns Green

8 **Partridge Green & Littleworth** (3 Pubs)

This walk is almost entirely level with the exception of a minor climb through woodland on section 2. I have only given it a two boot level of difficulty because some of the paths are a little uneven and can get a bit overgrown so more care is required.

The walk begins by passing the Partridge pub before heading out cross-country to reach the River Adur. After a short walk beside the river you reach Hatterell Bridge where you head back cross-country and through woodland to reach the Green Man. After another short trek cross-country you reach the Windmill before starting the final part of the walk down a lane back to the start.

Level: 🥾 🥾
Length: 4 miles (6.4 km)
Terrain: Mainly level but some paths are uneven and a little overgrown.
Stiles: 8
Park & start: Free car park in Village Hall Lane behind the Village Hall.
Postcode: RH13 8JY
Start ref: TQ 189192
Refreshments: Featured pubs.

① From the car park, go right down a 'No Entry' road passing the Village Hall on your right to reach the High Street – not signed. Turn right along the road to reach a main road at the end with the Partridge on the right.

The Windmill · 4
The Green Man · 3
Hatterell Bridge
B2135
① 🏠
The Partridge
Partridge Green
2

PARTRIDGE GREEN

Partridge Green derives its name from a family called Partrych who were registered in the area in 1332. In turn the name Partrych comes from the medieval word Petriche, which is the word for a 'snarer of partridges'. The settlement in what is now known as Partridge Green originated around the road junction of the B2135 / B2116 with several houses (in 1840 there were approximately six houses) and an inn called the Hare and Hounds. The Hare and Hounds was one of the meeting places for the West Grinstead Hundred court between 1786 and 1802. With the arrival of the railway the inn was replaced with a new building, the Station Inn (later Station Hotel). When the railway closed in 1966 it was renamed again as the Partridge.

The Partridge

Leave the pub, cross the main road and go left. In about 50 yards go right at a Public Bridleway / Downs Link sign. Follow the path and when you reach an access road by a 4-way footpath sign, go left. Follow the access road and at its end go through a swing gate on the right. In 10 yards, at a 3-way footpath sign, go left along a left field edge. In the field corner, go right next to a wire fence on the left.

Go through a swing gate and continue ahead. Go through another swing gate and continue ahead with a row of trees on your right. At the end of the trees, go ahead at a 2-way footpath sign along an overgrown and uneven path through scrub.

The path curves to the right to reach a stile. Cross the stile and continue along a right field edge. In the field corner, go left at a 2-way footpath sign and in 30 yards you reach the River Adur by a 2-way footpath sign.

2 Go right and walk with the river on your left. Just follow the path, with the river meandering away from you for a while, passing a footpath sign and crossing a stile / bridge. After the bridge, head slightly to the right on a clear path and then you arrive back beside the river. Soon

RIVER ADUR
The Adur is a river in Sussex which was formerly navigable by large ships up as far as Steyning where there was a large port, but over time the river valley became silted up and the port moved down to deeper waters nearer the mouth in Shoreham-by-Sea. The Adur starts as two separate branches, the western Adur and the eastern Adur, which meet just west of Henfield at Betley Bridge.

you reach a 4-way footpath sign at Hatterell Bridge.

Turn right and go through a wide metal gate into woodland. Follow the woodland path ahead, climbing gently. Go through a wide metal gate and ahead along a right field edge and then go across the middle of the next field on a wide grassy path. Go through a wooden bridle gate and ahead along a left field edge. Go through two wide metal gates, passing a 4-way footpath sign for the Downs Link in between.

Go ahead up a left field edge and in the far corner, cross a stile and continue ahead. At a junction of driveways, go ahead to reach a road. Turn right along the road for 30 yards to reach the Green Man pub on the right.

(3) Leave the pub and go left back along the road using the right hand pavement. Just before speed restriction signs and by a postbox on the right, go right through a swing gate next to a Public Footpath sign.

Hatterell Bridge

The Green Man

an enclosed path to reach Mill Lane — not signed.

Take a few paces to the left then go right over a stile at a footpath sign and follow the path to the left of a house. Cross another stile and go ahead up a left field edge to cross another stile and go right at a 3-way footpath sign. Follow the path which can get a little overgrown and taking extra care of the barbed-wire fence on your left. In view ahead of you is St Hugh's Carthusian Monastery at Parkminster in the parish of Cowfold.

Cross a stile and go along a left field edge then cross another stile and continue out to Littleworth Lane — not signed. Go right along the lane and in

Go along the right field edge, go through another swing gate and then go diagonally left across a playing field to the far corner. In the corner follow a clear path through a small area of trees and then continue along

The Windmill

along Oakwood. Follow it around to the left and then right. Cross St Michaels Way and continue to the next junction where you turn right along Little Oak. In 20 yards, go left along a road to arrive back at the car park on the right.

Millennium sign

a few yards you reach the Windmill pub on the right.

(4) Leave the pub and go right down the lane passing a

Millennium Littleworth sign on the right at the junction of Mill Lane. Just continue along the lane and soon you reach a sign for Partridge Green. Carry on and at a road junction, go right

9 Rusper & Lambs Green (3 Pubs)

This is an easy short walk at only 2.75 miles but it can be very interesting and a bit of fun. If you like pubs, photography or planes there is something for you but if you like all three – happy days – this walk could take you two to three hours. Rusper is very close to Gatwick Airport and there are aircraft constantly taking off next to you. Challenge yourself; try getting those perfect photographs using a hand-held camera on full zoom especially if you've already been to the pub.

The walk begins by the Plough Inn and heads out cross-country towards Lambs Green. On the way there are aircraft constantly flying overhead and the chance you may see deer if you are lucky. At Lambs Green you visit the Lamb Inn

Level: 🥾
Length: 2.75 miles (4.4 km)
Terrain: Mainly across fields with some minor inclines.
Stiles: 7
Park & start: Car park beside the church.
Postcode: RH12 4RA
Start ref: TQ 205372
Refreshments: Featured pubs.

before heading back to the Star Inn at Rusper. At the end (beginning) of the walk you pass the church of St Mary Magdalene; at the base of the tower, to the left of the church entrance, there is a plaque to a prioress and four nuns who were

re-interred here after their bodies were unearthed during the re-development of the twelfth century Rusper Priory.

RUSPER

The name derives from the Old English 'ruh spaer' which means 'rough enclosure'. In the twelfth century a Benedictine convent, Rusper Priory, was established in the parish. It closed in the seventeenth or eighteenth century and was finally demolished at the end of the eighteenth century. A new house was built on the site called The Nunnery and during construction the remains of a prioress and four nuns were uncovered; they were re-interred at the foot of the church tower.

The Plough Inn

① Leave the car park and walk across the road to the Plough Inn. Facing the Plough Inn, take the footpath which is a few yards to the right of the pub. Go through a swing gate and go ahead with trees / bushes on your left. Descend gradually and soon you go to the left of a paddock on an enclosed path as directed by a 2-way footpath sign. As you will

already have heard and seen by now there are plenty of aircraft to try and photograph.

Go through another swing gate and continue ahead between fields. At a gap in the trees you reach a 4-way footpath sign on the left; go right here with trees on your right.

Go through a gap in the trees and climb gently up a right field edge. In the far corner, go out to reach a road.

(2) Cross the road and continue ahead, to the left of a house, as directed by a footpath sign. Cross a stile and go along the right edge of a field. Cross a stile by a 2-way footpath sign and continue along an enclosed path; keep a look

out here as you may be lucky and see deer over on your left. When the enclosed path ends, go left at a footpath sign and follow a left field edge.

At a 2-way footpath sign go ahead with the wire fence on your left and the River Mole on your right. When the wire fence ends and with a metal

The Lamb Inn

gate ahead, go right through an opening by a 2-way footpath sign and follow the enclosed path out to Lambs Green Road, not signed. Go right along the quiet road and soon you reach the Lamb Inn on the left.

3 Leave the pub and continue left along the road for about 80 yards to reach a footpath sign on the right beside Canonbury Villas. Go right here and in a few yards go over a stile by a 2-way footpath sign, then diagonally left across a field.

Cross a bridge on the far side and go up the right edge of a field with trees on your right. As you climb the field you soon follow the path which takes you towards the far left corner of the field. In the field corner, go through a swing gate and follow the enclosed path out to a road.

Cross a stile opposite and go along the left edge of a field. Cross a stile in the field corner and continue ahead. In the field corner, go right through a wide metal gate (which will probably be open) and follow the obvious path up across a field, passing beneath power lines on the way.

At an opening by a 2-way footpath sign continue up between wooden fences. When you reach buildings at the top, go ahead over a stile by a 4-way footpath sign. Follow the enclosed path with houses on the left and soon you reach the car park for the Star Inn.

Go through the car park and visit the pub then continue along the road, passing the church of St Mary

Magdalene, back to the car park at the start.

The Star Inn

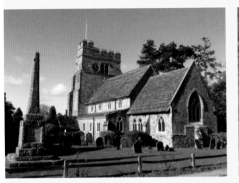

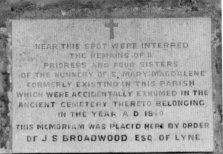

NEAR THIS SPOT WERE INTERRED
THE REMAINS OF A
PRIORESS AND FOUR SISTERS
OF THE NUNNERY OF S. MARY MAGDALENE
FORMERLY EXISTING IN THIS PARISH
WHICH WERE ACCIDENTALLY EXHUMED IN THE
ANCIENT CEMETERY THERETO BELONGING
IN THE YEAR A.D. 1840
THIS MEMORIAM WAS PLACED HERE BY ORDER
OF J S BROADWOOD ESQ OF LYNE

ST MARY MAGDALENE'S CHURCH

In 1975, Stephen Nightingale, a visiting boy scout, fell 70ft from the top of the tower and suffered only a broken arm. A popular belief is that the prayers of the nuns buried directly below the tower intervened to save him. A plaque at the base of the tower indicates the reburial of the nuns' remains, which had been disturbed by local rebuilding. Along with the nuns' bones was unearthed a unique chalice. It is now owned by the British Museum and is the earliest surviving example of a decorated 'Limoges' chalice in the Western Church.

10 **West Hoathly & Ardingly** (2 Pubs)

This 6 mile walk is very hilly and can get quite muddy, especially along the bridleways on section 2. West Hoathly is quite a remote village and is very elevated so your outward journey is predominantly downhill and

the return journey, section 3, is steeply uphill albeit up a quiet country lane.

The walk begins by the Cat Inn and St Margaret's church and heads out across fields before starting to descend down through woodland which has some interesting rock formations as well as an unusual water feature. At the end of the woodland you reach the main road with the Gardeners Arms pub and the South of England Centre on the opposite side; famous for the South of England Agricultural Show

Level: 🥾 🥾 🥾
Length: 6 miles (9.7 km)
Terrain: A very hilly walk throughout. Section 3 is almost entirely uphill albeit along a lane. Parts of the walk can get very muddy.
Stiles: 8
Park & start: Roadside parking by the church / Cat Inn.
Postcode: RH19 4PP
Start ref: TQ 362325
Refreshments: Featured pubs.

and often used for antiques fairs which are featured on the BBC game show *Bargain Hunt*. The return journey is steeply up a quiet lane for about 1.5 miles to arrive at the Priest House Museum back in West Hoathly.

WEST HOATHLY

The area was already settled by the eleventh century, when St Margaret's church was founded. At that time the village was known as Hadlega and Hodlega, later standardised to Hodlegh and Hothelegh, then (West) Hoathly. This Anglo-Saxon word signifies a heath-covered clearing.

St Margaret's church

① Facing The Cat Inn, go left over a stile which is beside a covered wooden bus stop next to a 3-way footpath sign. Go ahead along a wide grassy path and soon you go through an open gate or over a stile to the right of it. Continue along the right edge of a field with trees on your right.

In the field corner, go ahead along the next right field edge, as directed by an arrow on a marker post, still with trees on your right. In the field corner, go along a short track then continue ahead along a road soon passing two cottages on the left. The road starts to descend and in about 50 yards you reach a few more houses by a 3-way footpath sign.

(2) Go left along an access track and where it bends to the right; go ahead over two stiles in quick succession as directed by 2-way footpath signs. Start off across the centre of a large field then aim for a stile in the far right corner by a 2-way footpath sign.

Go over the stile and diagonally right through trees for a few yards, then cross a sleeper bridge over Cob Brook. Cross a stile by a 2-way footpath sign and go right along the right edge of a field with trees on your right. Just follow the field edge then go left, by a 2-way footpath sign within the same field, still with trees on your right.

Cross a stile and continue ahead to cross another stile (watch you footing on the other side of this stile as it is very uneven) into woodland. In a few yards, at a 2-way footpath sign, go diagonally left to another 2-way footpath sign then go right, down and over a bridge.

Four yards after the bridge, go left up a narrow and uneven path and in a few yards go up four steps and ahead with houses on your left. Just follow this uneven and slightly overgrown path until you reach a 3-way footpath sign by a bridge. Go right here and follow the path down through woodland passing an unusual water feature on the right.

At the end of the path you reach a 3-way bridleway sign. Go ahead here

Water feature in woodland.

Rock/tree formation

and follow the wide track, passing some interesting rock / tree formations on the right as you go.

Just follow the wide path and at an opening there is a 3-way bridleway sign. Continue ahead and in a few yards you pass another 2-way bridleway sign before continuing along a winding enclosed path which can get very muddy.

The path re-enters woodland and soon starts to climb. At a 3-way bridleway sign, go right to reach the main road. (If you do not want to visit the pub go to section 3 and continue ahead here to reach Cob Lane.) Turn right along the road with the South of England Centre on the left and the Gardeners Arms about 200 yards along on the right.

3   Leave the pub and turn left, back along the main road to reach the bridleway you used to get here. Go back down the bridleway to reach the 3-way bridleway sign and go right, down through woodland. Soon you reach Cob Lane, not signed.

ARDINGLY

Ardingly (pronounced 'Arding-lye') is a village in the High Weald Area of Outstanding Natural Beauty. It is famous for Wakehurst Place and its grounds which are 1.5 miles north of the village and referred to as 'Kew in the Country', and for Ardingly Reservoir which is 1 mile west of the village. Each year in early June the Ardingly Showground (South of England Centre) hosts the famous South of England Agricultural Show and is often used for antiques fairs which are frequently featured on the BBC game show Bargain Hunt. *The Gardeners Arms pub is located on the opposite side of the road to both Wakehurst Place and Ardingly Showground.*

Cob Brook

Go left along the very quiet lane, soon crossing Cob Brook.

Just follow the lane for about 1.5 miles, climbing all the way steeply at first, back towards West Hoathly. At West Hoathly you follow the lane around to the right, passing the West Hoathly Bowls Centre on the right and the Priest House Museum on the left. Continue for a few more yards back to the start.

PRIEST HOUSE MUSEUM

The Priest House, opposite St Margaret's church, was turned into a museum by the Sussex Archaeological Society in 1935. The fifteenth-century open hall-house, with a five-bay façade and a solar wing, retains some original windows and its king post (central vertical supporting post) and trussed roof. Inside there are items relating to local and domestic history and there are formal gardens.